Goest

Cole Swensen

Alice James Books
Farmington, Maine

10 9 8 7 6 5 4 3 2

Alice James Books are published by Alice James Poetry Cooperative, Inc., an affiliate of the
University of Maine at Farmington.

Alice James Books
238 Main Street
Farmington, ME 04938

www.alicejamesbooks.org

Library of Congress Cataloging-in-Publication Data
Swensen, Cole
Goest / Cole Swensen.
    p.   cm.
ISBN 1-882295-43-9
I. Title.
PS3569.W384G64 2004
811'.54—dc22   2003024339

Alice James Book gratefully acknowledges support from the University of Maine at Farmington
and the National Endowment for the Arts. 🌱

Art Credit: Christo and Jeanne-Claude: Running Fence, Sonoma and Marin Counties, California,
1972–76. 5.5 Meters (18 feet) high. 39.4 kilometers (24 ½ miles) long. Copyright © Christo 1976.
Photo: Jeanne-Claude.

Goest

Also by Cole Swensen:

Such Rich Hour

Oh

Try

Noon

Numen

Park

New Math

It's Alive She Says

Reading Robert Ryman (chapbook)

And Hand (chapbook)

O (chapbook)

Translations

Future, Former, Fugitive by Olivier Cadiot

OXO by Pierre Alferi

Island of the Dead by Jean Frémon

Bayart by Pascalle Monnier

Art Poetic' by Olivier Cadiot

Natural Gaits by Pierre Alferi

Acknowledgments

My warm thanks to the editors and staffs of the following publications in which these poems first appeared (sometimes in earlier versions) for their generous support of this work and of contemporary poetry in general.

American Letters & Commentary: "Things to Do with Naphtha," "The Development of Natural Gas"

Aufgabe: "Future White"

Bellingham Review: "What the Ventriloquists Intended," "The Origin of *Ombres Chinoises*," "The Discovery of Bologna Stone"

Canary River Review: "The Game of Balls and Cups"

Colorado Review: "Others," "Five Landscapes"

Conduit: "The Invention of Automata," "The Invention of the Pencil," "The Invention of the Hydrometer"

Conjunctions: "The History of Artificial Ice," "The Lives of Saltpeter," "Lacrymae Vitrae"

Crowd: "The Razed Cities," "The Invention of the Weathervane"

DIA Foundation: "White Cities"

Electronic Poetry Review: "The Invention of Streetlights"

Idiom: "The Future of Sculpture"

Iowa City Arts Council Poetry in Public Project: "The Girl Who Never Rained"

Ploughshares: "The Invention of the Night-watch," "The Invention of Mirror," "The Invention of Incised Glass"

Shiny: "Five Landscapes"

Vagant (in Norwegian translation): "The Invention of Streetlights," "The Lives of Saltpeter"

And many thanks to the Pushcart Press for choosing "Five Landscapes" for a Pushcart Prize, and to Bruce Beasley for nominating it.

I would also like to thank Cal Bedient and Nicole Terry for their invaluable feedback, and Stefanie Marlis and Cort Day for the same.

Section Two is based on *A History of Inventions, Discoveries, and Origins* by John Beckmann, 4th edition, published by Henry Bohn, London, 1846.

Most of the italicized passages in "The Future of Sculpture" and "The Future of White" are taken from the titles of or inscriptions on Cy Twombly's sculptures. My thanks to him for these words, and for every aspect and each instance of all of his works.

Contents

to Anthony Hayward

Life is not a personal thing.

—Gilles Deleuze

1

Of White

The Girl Who Never Rained

Oddly enough, there was always a city block of clear weather on every side of her, a space just large enough that the casual passerby simply thought, "What an odd spot of calm," and often even people who knew her well never quite put it together, as, after all, it's not that unusual to have a break in a storm, though they'd develop, after a while, an odd inclination to be with her without really thinking out why. Other than that, her life was neither better nor worse than most, except, of course, for the crowds.

Others

You walk into a house
in which several people are sitting in the dark
around a dinner table, eating, drinking, laughing.

Every night on the answering machine
there is, among the others,
one blank call, at least thirty seconds of nothing;
if it ever stopped, you'd have to start
calling up and leaving it
for someone else.

There's a set of identical twins who communicate through prime numbers, and certain figures in medieval paintings whose extra fingers can only be seen at a glance.

Once there was a man
who wrote a symphony based entirely
on the arrangement of birds on the power lines outside;
it's called solmifying—*to solmizate* in the infinitive; transitive: to sing
any object into place.

In the crowded subway, a stranger stands behind you with one hand firmly, warmly, on the small of your back.

Niepce's first photograph,
which was the first photograph,
was of a scene of roofs so blurred they were often mistaken for sails.

Or people passing

on the other side of frosted glass,

a woman at the opera is talking in her sleep.

Once there was a man who sang in his sleep.

Four out of five living things are insects.

Five Landscapes

One

Green moves through the tops of trees and grows
lighter greens as it recedes, each of which includes a grey, and among the
greys, or beyond them, waning finely into white, there is one white spot,
absolute; it could be an egret or perhaps a crane at the edge of the water
where it meets a strip of sand.

Two

There is a single, almost dazzling white spot of a white house out loud
against the fields, and the forest in lines
receding, rises,
and then planes. Color,

in pieces or entire; its presence
veneers over want; in all its moving parts, it could be something else

half-hidden by trees. Conservatory, gloriette, gazebo, or bandshell,
a door ajar on the top floor.

Three

The trees are half air. They fissure the sky; you could count the leaves, pare
time
                  defined as that which,
                  no matter how barely, exceeds
                  what the eye could grasp in a glance:
intricate woods opening out before a body of water edged
with a swatch of meadow where someone has hung a bright white sheet
out in the sun to dry.

Four

A white bird in a green forest is a danger to itself. Stands out. Shines. Builds
up inside. Like it's dangerous to cry while driving or to talk to strangers or to
stare at the sun and a thousand other things
                                                          we've always heard
people who wear white see better at night, though they gradually lose this
trait as they age.

Five

The air across the valley is slightly hazy though thinning though patches remain between the groves of trees that edge a clearing in which stands a single house. A child in a white t-shirt has just walked out of the house and is turning to walk down to the lake.

The Future of Sculpture

Cy Twombly, Sculptures, National Gallery, Washington DC, 2001

The Future of Light

Give the box

back to the weal (the sun peeled) to a line, which is thin, to a dim
Give it back to him.
As the white brush brushes over you again you are counting time run
into the sun (until it equals)

                                   Throw the sun into the box.
The box is painted white. By your own hand
the sun was hauled into view and proved to be
a pale thing off which the paint is flaking.

                In Time the Wind Will Come and Destroy my Lemons
                Rome 1987

Everything white is turning
into a white wall
           And we

who always thought of happiness climbing
Rome, 1974.

Or *Madame d'O,* Jupiter Island
with the words inside it
and the little key unlocked
in place. States "the fragile arrangement of the world"
is a face
painted white
on a stage
soaring.   We draped the stage in sheets
                   and nailed it into place. And put a lightbulb inside it
and said that it bloomed

too soon. *The Future of Sight*
                              who bore,
it was said, a clear and colorless fruit. Put
it in the box.
                    His hands of sufficient cause
and of all he touched, it is said

                    the Red Sea is white, and the Dead Sea, dead. Is a thread
seen end on—kingdom, phylum, class, and duress
is of the vast.
                    And then a chariot runs through it. *Car nymphea caerulea*
Toys are ancient children.

White Cities

as they recede

into the blazing city

that all the white boats are leaving, a city sailing
into ages, please repeat:

1) The city is white.
2) Most cities are white.
3) The white thing you see if you turn around quickly

often far away, often far out to sea, though at times across a plain,
a shimmer, or as if silt falling, fine-grained, a counting sand, a seed
well-timed

1) made of talc
2) made of chalk
3) made of sugar, which melts in the sun. This is a city on which the sun
pours down.

A man in passing glanced in a window, and all he'd ever seen was there. In
the next street, a boy walked along, counting the cobblestones: One, one,
one, one, one.

2

A History of the Incandescent

Lacrymae Vitreae

*the rapid cooling of this extraordinary glass drop leaves it
in a state of enormous tension . . . —Jane Draycott*

For the fabrication of artificial tears, John Christian Schulenburg, 1695,
sent a bitter silicate
                to brittle it   to thin air
                And dropped from there to fusing water
                                      the entire
seventeenth century tier after tier
                on the terrace of the boat on which it was escorted
                from Sweden to Paris will just shatter

and "must excite the curiosity of philosophers"
They succeeded best with green glass yet

        to withstand the most ardent blow
      at the thick end while the thin
      reverts to sand at the slightest tap: this crack
in an otherwise temperate state:
                        scientists will note
we, who were all home at the time,
                  bursting into finest dust
if even the smallest fragment is broken off.

The Invention of the Night-watch

All dark walks   it's in all the books—Psalms, Solomon,
                                 the ones with all the pictures
crossed out. A legion of staves, and etched onto the leaves: what here
I have witnessed

a blind world kinder
beneath a torch
held in a sheaf
on which said *eye* and *yes*
                 On which said light is fixed,
                       while in the molten light they stood

                       on corners all night long as the bell-bearers stalked
abroad and what you thought was a tolling of the hours you were counting
was in fact an encoded reporting of events: theft, murder, fire, wolf, circle
one
is worthy of attention, is

and then we were eaten. 1385.   There's a light that lists toward each en
                                route to heaven and we follow the
                                folding screens. Between seven and
                                sixteen bodies a night were collected off
                                the streets of Paris from the thirteenth
                                through the seventeenth centuries and
                                several more from the Seine.
                                Who counted in his sleep
counted his sleep;
who took a walk after dark, *I have a friend*
in the world.

The Invention of Streetlights

>   *noctes illustratas*
>   (the night has houses)

and the shadow of the fabulous
broken into handfuls—these
can be placed at regular intervals,
candles
walking down streets at times eclipsed by trees.

Certain cells, it's said, can generate light on their own.

There are organisms that could fit on the head of a pin
and light entire rooms.

Throughout the Middle Ages, you could hire a man
on any corner with a torch to light you home

                              were lamps made of horn
and from above a loom of moving flares, we watched
Notre Dame seem small.
Now the streets stand still.

By 1890, it took a pound of powdered magnesium
to photograph a midnight ball.

While as early as 50 BCE, riotous soldiers leaving a Roman bath
sliced through the ropes that hung the lamps from tree to tree
                              and aloft us this
                              new and larger room
Flambeaux the arboreal
                              was the life of Julius Caesar
              in whose streets
              in which a single step could be heard.
We opened all our windows
and looked out on a listening world laced here and there with points of light,
                    Notre Dame of the Unfinished Sky,
oil slicks burning on the river; someone down on the corner
striking a match to read by.

Some claim Paris was the first modern city to light its streets.
    The inhabitants were ordered
       in 1524 to place a taper in every window in the dark there were 912 streets
              walked into this arc until by stars
              makes steps sharp, you are
         and are not alone
by public decree
October 1558: the lanterns were similar to those used in mines:
"Once
we were kings"
              and down into the spiral of our riches
still reign: *falots* or great vases of pitch lit
at the crossroads
        —and thus were we followed
                    through a city of thieves—which,
but a few weeks later, were replaced by chandeliers.

While others claim all London was alight by 1414.

There it was worded:

Out of every window, come a wrist with a lanthorn

                            and were told

                            hold it there

             and be on time

and not before

and watched below

the faces lit, and watched the faces pass.   And turned back in

(the face goes on) and watched the lights go out.

Here the numbers are instructive:

               In the early 18th century, London hung some 15,000 lamps.

And now we find (1786) they've turned to crystal, placed precisely,

each its own distance, small in islands, large in the time it would take to run.

And Venice started in 1687 with a bell

upon the hearing of which, we all in unison
exit,
match in hand, and together strike them against an upper tooth and touch
the tiny flame to anything, and when times get rough (crime up, etc.) all we
have to do is throw oil out upon the canals to make the lighting uncommonly
extensive. Sometimes we do it just to shock the rest of Europe, and at other
times because we find it beautiful.

Says Libanius
       Night differs us
            Without us
            noctes illustratas
               Though in times of public grief
when the streets were left unlit, on we went, just
dark marks in the markets and voices in the cafes, in the crowded squares,
a single touch, the living, a lantern
               swinging above the door any time a child is born, be it
Antioch, Syria, or Edessa—
and then there were the festivals,
          the *festum encaeniorum,* and others in which
          they call idolatrous, these torches
                    half a city wide
                       be your houses.

The First Lightbulb

precise erase

a gate again
where the sky died
in a coin

The History of Artificial Ice

"We hear that in Persia they are feasting on ice"

                             though how they managed it remains obscure.
We know it took trenches ten feet deep and people paid to walk all night
as long as the night was clear.
The recipe claimed

                         and still we worked
to refract each drop through a living cell. And were told

Go from water to gold in a single leap and the ice will lie
suspended between. A prism

                           makes the sun go cold. I hang it in a window
in its little cubes.
                         until Aristotle modernized the process
by suggesting lead. You throw it in in pieces (Plutarch also said this) I have
found a frosted city that will not come down.

                             "I cannot find

in this circumference"

the word *glacière* in any dictionary before
                    They smuggled the jewels out in snow
                    and naturally confused the two.
                    Constantinople, 1553: sorbet served
nightly on the lighted terrace: Tuesdays it was green; Thursdays, yellow
because the boats arrived in tandem, and by Sunday it was orange.

The Invention of the Hydrometer

The letters rest upon the desk, and next to them
a series of fluids:

                    to fall into liquid masses;
to raw the gravity of axes

                          first tested by weighing the crown of Hiero
which put it in a useful perspective. The first letter says
Dear Hypatia
(d. 415) who would have been a saint
had she only been a Christian, was seized in the street, stripped and shredded

and dragged her fractured limbs until all her brilliant math had drained from
them. Into the umpteenth letter from the bishop Synesius, in which we read:

Dear Hypatia, please
make for me

           a hydrometer
           the size and shape of a reed. And I quote: "A line drawn upon it
is intersected by selected others, and these reveal the weight of water"

who in turn betrayed her when he thought
he was just turning around to answer

                              She wrote
You forgot.

Hypatia, *please*.

                Fermat tried, but couldn't reconcile the versions.
                Any liquid can be weighed by its resistance;
it's like falling into history, which misses you.

The Invention of the Mirror

"And therein found this face"

there at the bottom

      something moving through the tarnish
at a different rate.
           They poured the liquid metal
across the flattened panes. Ice upon ice: antimony,
lead, colophonium
          once called mirror-resin
(now used only for violins) and tin, hammered into leaves
and over it poured mercury, rubbed in by heel of hand, foot of hare

and at the back, a shadow at the back
of the eye in great sheets would orbit like a moon,
said Johannes Peckham
        or Peccam
        who taught at Oxford, Paris, and Rome,
            and if the lead were removed
the face would disappear, said Philolaus the Pythagorean who believed
the sun a vitreous body
        oddly
built of cast-off centuries with all their pictures in place.

Though if the sun itself is a mirror

                              just think:

                              it's a single step—

                                             slip

                       and the glass comes back

inhabited

                       Empedocles said

              which Eusebius compares

to a reflection on water

                       Who was it

thought the sun transparent

                       and all the earth a lens? said

              the body of the brittle

                              stares back,

swears

the image can't be shaken, and even when broken

it does not necessarily follow that

the face too is glass.

In France, mirrors were made in great galleries called *serres,*
                                    or in the infinitive, *serrer,*
which can mean to grip
                        if bird of prey, or in greenhouses, pane after pane,
set out in the blazing sun to temper
but instead they grew: 1688:
                Abraham Thevart cast plates eighty-four inches high and
fifty wide, but stretched so thin, they'd shatter when you picked them up,
and there you'd be with a mirror the size of your thumb and fit entirely therein.
                                    They did not survive.
                                Nitrate of silver
                        spirit of hartshorn
                    and a couple ounces of water.
Let stand 24 hours,
                    then oil of cassia, then of clove and polish
with lateral strokes. We have skated
right past the marvel, beyond the threshold
of surface tension, jotted in the margin *Yet they fill us with dread.*

The New World

Used flint
          or an obsidian strain.
They had others made of Inca stone
said by Ulloa to have been

blue and crossed by veins
that take no polish, that break
in sequence   or pyrite
               or marcasite
          sometimes called the stone of health
worn in a ring
so that with a single downward glance you can be
the infinitesimal:
                    Sing:
                    if in pieces
                    we are accurate
here the *we* accrues.

The Invention of the Weathervane

Mapping wind back to anchor
           in a harbor city
           or farther, insisted,
                      the glorious fleet off Normandy, 1013,
                      was led by birds on edge
on a mast, steel wind.

Wind must be sewn separately into every direction, the needles in rhythm, invisible
in the tapestry at Bayeaux, the birds, defiant,
                            hold their own against entire seas.

Cicero knew wind better than he knew birds, and so resolved to embark.

Thus the anemoscope:
birds born with four wings, all angled off each other to suggest a circle,
and all signaling shore: "There is no shore here." A severed storm, a bird
with many tongues. We've counted twelve winds, but the tongues split.

The Invention of Automata

Perhaps simply from nostalgia
                              and a love of things that interlock:

John Müller's iron dragonfly, who flew, and his artificial eagle, who went out ahead to meet the Emperor Maximilian, June 7, 1470. And a wild duck that could fly, eat, and cry all at once, driven by a system of interlocking chains, and a peacock on St. Christopher Island, who, it's said, could sing. All these marvels ran like a common pocket watch, which wasn't all that common then

and are, I think, related to the case of Wolgamot, the Englishman, who made his name training bees, who walked about the countryside covered with them, even to his face and hands, and caressed them and let them drink from his eyes.

What the Ventriloquists Said

amid the growing craze for automatons
The voice within the device that moves   is not
(as if nothing human
could be quite that moving) My precious edgling: *though*
some
believe
the answers be given by a man concealed,
these are speaking machines.

They were risking their lives.
Usually a woman or a child, who woke up inside the oracle,
who swallowed the burning oil, and who forces the idols to speak?

Though when the bishop Theophilus
broke open the statues at Alexandria, he found them hollow

it does not necessarily follow that

The penalty for trickery was death.
Such is the wealth of belief.
Behind a finely painted sheet of shell
a voice unlatched surrounds the world.

The Origin of *Ombres Chinoises*

In the physics of the whisper, this gallery of asias, I've seen them
                                rising fan-shaped through lacquer
and later at the feast of lanterns, says Prosper Alpinus, 1735:
                                It takes a whole circus:
                                You stand the figures in a circle
and behind each one, a person
                        the light shines through
                                to the opposite wall
                                and the specters thereon,
                        though the earliest treatises say *spectators,*
and that the wall was gauze, and the first performance occurred
when a hand moving in to guard a flame
caught and headed off on its own.
                                There are screens behind which
everything goes ancient
                        and born of these shades, contagious; they make us
more numerous in silence.

The Game of Balls and Cups

Just turn them upside down
                              and the flicker slips
among, unseen,
                        is one of the oldest
          acres of magic
(under which we are hiding) Slide me
                              from one to one
And the other who stayed behind in the theater repeating "make of this
                        my country"

                        Or else they used shells and a pearl

and called them *calculi* —"small-ball-
never-where-you-think-I-am."
                              have been found engraved
on the tomb of Baqt III at Beni Hassan, 2500 BCE
                        and everywhere between
                        who believed
that even little flights must have insides
                              turned infinite when the cup is lifted
even if
they too must be of countable number. In this tent in the distance, come
into my tent of numbers. Count them.

The Discovery of Bologna Stone

And all because it shines in the dark.

It was an accident. Once there was

a shoemaker (1603) in search of gold

and most of what we know about light

is the color of water
                    woven without us, our *lapis solaris*
foliaceous in structure
                    and no one in the town would say a thing.

There are magnets for light. They enter the darkened room.
You pound the stone to a paste and shape it like a sun.
There's no magic to this. You leave it in the sun
and it *lumens*, then it *fugits*, and then (it is written)
if not the magnet, then the siren: *pyrophorus*
as presented to King Henri II of France
on his way to reclaim the throne, a stranger offered him a stone on fire but
he saw the danger and turned away in time. Will the light come back. Will the
altered room, will the colors in their sequence become confused. Especially
after heavy rains, when it pours down the hillside in streams, and If, In fact,
there's nothing that can turn a stone to gold
                                        I keep the rest
in a box above the door to guard the dark.

Things to Do with Naphtha

They called it the blood of Nessus
and went dressed in it, ancestors of our friends
who step off curbs and burst into flame. It's how Medea destroyed Creusa.
Even Alexander the Great said "Oh my

                                        proximate annihilette, come closer
to this candle. We've rubbed the walls with sulphur
and
                                This is how the rabbi Bar-Cocheba
                                in the reign of Hadrian
                                appeared as the messiah. How
the emperor Constantine, terror-struck
lit a cigarette, despite
all we've heard we don't expect a flame to grow in air that just seconds before
yet in Valentinian's case, his own bodyguards inhaled a blaze and
exhaled a conflagration.
                                Why wake him?

Of Manganese and Other Things

In iron is the seed of sky.
        We stumble into brilliance, and if we're lucky, we remember
what the stone looked like.

A bit magnetic.

While others turned to thinking glass
                is mined from sand
                     as silver
is from rock, and from there conjectured:
                Manganese can call forth rain
from deep inside a tree, and luminous fish from the sea,
                    said Pliny, who
never quite believed
        claimed Albertus Magnus, who used the example
of a compass: See—
        it sets sail in all its blues and greens, and if I have indulged
in these observations, it is only to suggest that a calcareous earth
worked
     as did the false notions of Kepler:
                let A be the axis, and thus the masses
found comfort.
    It was not a magnet. It called nothing forth.
     And if, when used as a glaze, it cures the plague, It's an accident,
or so they claimed
who ate chalk raw, walked clothed in mica scraps, and in so many ways
were added sparingly to molten glass to make it clear as glass.

The Lives of Saltpeter

Glass made its first appearance
on the shores outside of Belus
        when sailors placed blocks of saltpeter under cooking pots
        causing the sand to fuse along the entire edge of the sea
ran another sea that refused to move

has been proved false. It simply wouldn't have worked.
        We use it, said Virgil
        to bring forth fruit.
Others: to preserve the dead.
        And even today there are places
where they wash their hands in potash as a kind of prayer
        aqua regia
        to lixiviate the nitrous particles
is but a child's game.
        Trace it back to Avicenna, who called it *sal alchali:*
        "Oh my soda and woodash,
        my natrum and borith,
        that traceth
a silk route right on through it: Al kali: *Who shall stand when he appeareth?*
        We offer:
        aquafortis,
        anamnesis,
        the clean from the unclean, undressing.

Which all boils down to salt, or to a single salt, or to all salts that
once cut right, keep on cutting inside. They sailed vessels of nitre,
                     They say the candelabra,
        They want for none other
                   and drink from that in which their lilies stand
in the rock-salt of pure crystal,
                 and looked it. This that
                 melts in the hand
                        (which and?
                            of his own account
somehow ended in gunpowder.

The Invention of Etched, Engraved & Incised Glass

To break the surface tension, yet maintain suspension,
        as if a feather had been inserted
                or a wheel hovered
                lightly by. It was a diamond
that first wrote on glass, in fact it was
                     François I, 16th c., idly etching women
are fickle into the pane with his ring as he stood gazing
out over the river, a sheet of blank water, a will
this diamond ring engender
              and that which changed it
              changèd were
              for diamond is to ocean
              what clustered frost on crystal:
Venice, 1562: drinking watercolor wine from an aviary in flight
and by 1670:
        aquafortis meritas florus all over the windows
flowering animals

were for decades kept secret

                        or at least the process
                        veiled; the figures rising

by themselves; the recipe: *ply*

                        with strong fire, toss

into pulverized Bohemian emerald also called

hesphorus, which

when reduced to a powder and heated

emits a green light over darkness   is brittle

                        air

                        is shining sere, is

                        and grows

vines and wings and all living windows

                        looking out on the river and its patterns.

The Exploration of Fluor-Spar

"Many beautiful colors can only, as we know,
be brought forth by means of fire."

Theophrastus claimed he knew
certain stones that turn to water when added to copper, silver, or iron
and a kind of solid fluor-spar that, though fragile,
had a greenish glow refracted against its inner walls

that rang

and poured

as avid ore
who, said Elsholz: 1676, ever thought a rock could melt

had known

stone lit by neither sun nor fire that when heated on metal
glowed milk-blue and scattered, suddenly powdered
into luminous letters in the hands of Leibniz, all vessels and vases,
if heated too quickly, flee, though they say *flieht,* and that it's never more
half-open than a door.

The Invention of the Pencil

        a mark upon parchment increases the window
or may even be
        the window behind which a swaying branch appears human.

Ambrosinus with his *lapis plumbarius* who traveled throughout Europe
tracing behind him a thin dark line.
        What will not come back.
        Crucible and pit.
        When burned
leaves nothing but a little iron and a silicate earth.

They tried others: *nigrica fabrilis,* which breaks on touch;
        matita nera, also known as black chalk:
            to make a body of every mark,
they said, slightly shaking their heads as they sewed in the sun,
to replace the silent flight of a stylus
        fade. Even Vasari

envied the feathered edge, the infinite greys. We aim a bit of graphite
at vellum and it stains. Beyond every window is a line where the world starts.

The Development of Natural Gas

And the lamps will grow in number

        There's a button factory in Birmingham using it to solder
A single cotton mill in Manchester
          with over a thousand burners
                          in a detailed account
                      of the coal fields of China
              while drilling even deeper
          the flames some 20 or 30 feet high
once harnessed, boiled the water from the salt, while
what remained, remained as light, a lucent fringe
to the hand that turned
          the valve to red
       in 1803
the Lyceum Theater in London was illuminated by gas, and a few years later,
the street outside it,
a curved street lined with trees, or is that simply
a trick of memory with its variable eye
           forced upward in jets
                until you washed it till it burned

           turned to millions
crushed beneath the weight, sold their matches
outright on the street, from Mayfair to Vauxhall
          All phosphor be with you.

3

On White

Razed Cities

There can be no gesture now

that does not incorporate (i.e. *to bring into the body of*)

the body, moving outward; there can be

no gesture

 inward.

The city stands on a single finger. Where is the photograph

that shows

the one apartment block left standing

right in the middle

he took the paintings out of the closet

and lined them along the wall.

The first thing I do whenever I move is paint the walls all white.

There's a painting of this

she said pointing to the photograph, "It's perfectly white."

"You mean it's blank?" "No, white."

"You mean there's nothing there?" "Then who are they?"

The Future of White

Cy Twombly, Sculptures; National Gallery, Washington D.C. 2001

Wheel
          my folded wheel; wheel that works
behind the circle

          circles now, *Ionian Sea*

          my box of dead

we left   spread out
               while among the reeds, bleached:
                                   the palm
                         that wouldn't set.
               Wrap up well.
               When happiness falls
               and we look up startled
               at the soft white curve

          Orphée

          and they

will be the crucial bridge, stitched, its lanterns fired
with flour and dust. A woman dressed
in a ziggurat walks in and simply sits down. This was
the war; this is how
we got here, this
house
this living wall with all its doorknobs on.
White tower
White tune
and a couple red lines you can't quite read.
They say *"Rome"* and

"if"
and
"and"
We left

them their dead as a gift.

We, who have always thought
once this white, the shapes would live themselves to life,

O little wheel with tiny teeth.

Five Landscapes

One

I'm on a train, watching landscape streaming by, thinking
of the single equation that lets time turn physical,
equivocal, almost equable on a train

where a window is speed, *vertile, vertige*. It will be

one of those beautiful equations, almost visible, almost green. There

in the field, a hundred people, a festival, a lake, a summer, a
hundred thousand fields, a woman
places her hand on the small of a man's back in the middle of the crowd
and leaves it.

Two

A wedding in a field—the old saying: it's good luck to be seen
in white from a train. You must be looking the other way; so many things
work only if you're looking away. A woman in a field is walking away.
Gardens early in the evening. Trees
planted a few hundred years ago to line a road no longer there.
There's a lake, pale teal; its light, field after field. Spire, steeple, sea

of trees that line roads long disappeared along with their houses, which were
great houses in their time.

Three

A vineyard unleashed. The varieties of green. One glances accidently
into entire lives: plumage, habitat, and distance between
the girl raising her head, turning to her friend
lost under the trees—you say it was a ring?
Engraved, the birds rise up from the field like grain
thrown. Into a line of birds planing just above the wheat.

Four

Each scene, as accidental as it is inevitable, so visibly, you look out on, say
a field, say leaves, with a river on the other side, another life, identical
but everyone's this time. Trees in a wallpaper pattern. An horizon
of dusk that barely outruns us. He started with pages and pages

and then erased. This one
will have a thousand pictures.

A field of houses pierced by windows.

Five

There's a wedding in a field I am passing in a train
                                          a field
in the green air, in the white air, an emptier here
                                          the field is everywhere
because it looks like something similar somewhere else.

Recent Titles from Alice James Books

Alice James Books has been publishing exclusively poetry since 1973. One of the few presses in the country that is run collectively, the cooperative selects manuscripts for publication through both regional and national annual competitions. New regional authors become active members of the cooperative, participating in the editorial decisions of the press. The press, which historically has placed an emphasis on publishing women poets, was named for Alice James, sister of William and Henry, whose fine journal and gift for writing went unrecognized within her lifetime.

DESIGNED BY MIKE BURTON

PRINTED BY THOMSON SHORE